SELLING SPELLING TO KIDS

Motivating games and activities to reinforce spelling skills

by
Imogene Forte
and
Mary Ann Pangle

Incentive Publications, Inc.
Nashville, Tennessee

Cover and illustrations by Becky Cutler

ISBN 0-86530-060-7

TABLE OF CONTENTS

PREFACE

Oh, no! It's spelling time again! In too many elementary classrooms today this expresses the attitudes of both teachers and students. Weekly lists, workbooks and/or highly structured language programs have taken all the fun out of teaching and learning spelling skills.

No one is advocating a return to the days of the blue-back speller and the Friday spelldown. There is however, something to be said for the motivation afforded by a common sense approach to the development of basic spelling skills. This book is a collection of games and activities to make spelling easier and more relevant to everyday life. Its purpose is to help teachers make spelling programs come alive in their own classrooms, and to encourage boys and girls to become personally involved in spontaneous language learning experiences.

The games and activities have been planned to meet the needs and interests of students with differing abilities, and to be implemented in a variety of classroom settings. Their use is limited neither to traditional, open space nor any other organizational arrangement. Many are adaptable for small or large group use, and some may be used for either enrichment or tutorial purposes by an individual student.

Game boards and activities have been designed to be easily produced, stored and implemented. The materials necessary for their construction have been limited to those readily available in most classrooms and call for no special artistic ability. In many instances, students themselves will want to become involved in the selection and preparation of materials most appropriate to their own unique needs and interests.

We hope this collection will help "sell spelling" to the teachers and students who use it.

Imogene Forte
Mary Ann Pangle

VOWEL VOYAGE

Purpose:

Using long and short vowels

Preparation:

1. Provide construction paper, scissors, crayons and a die.

2. Reproduce a copy of the game board on the following page.

Procedure:

1. This game is for two, three or four players.

2. Each player designs a marker, cuts it out of construction paper and then places it on the game board.

3. The first player throws the die and moves the correct number of spaces. If the die lands on a space marked "ă," the player must spell a word that contains a short "a" sound. If the word is misspelled, the player must go back one space and so on.

4. The other players continue until one player goes around the board three times to win the game.

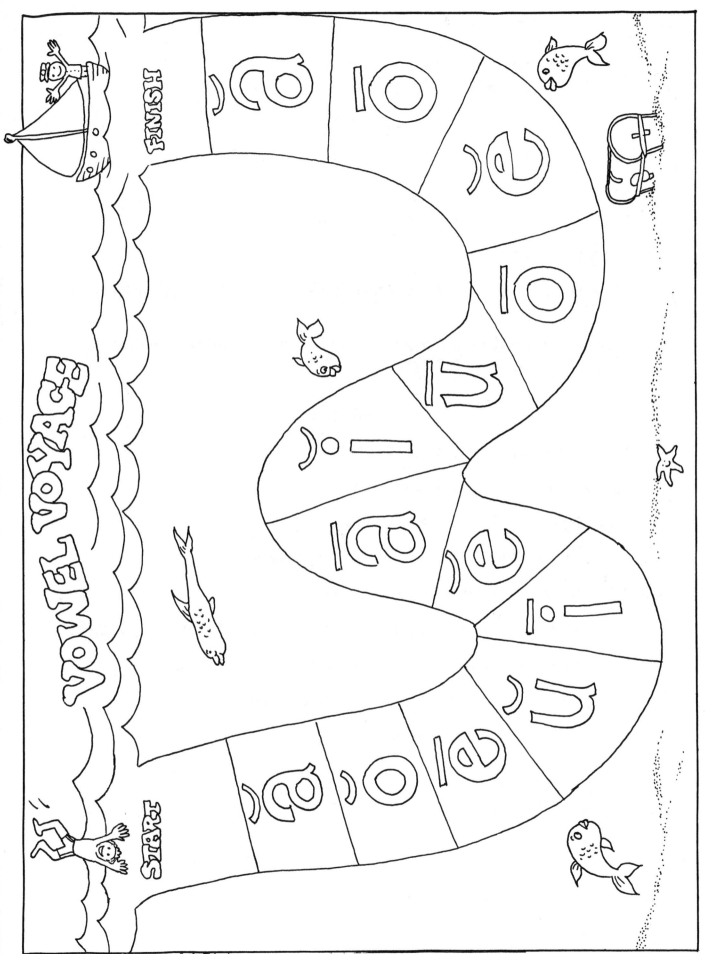

9

PICK POCKET

Purpose:

Using vowels

Preparation:

1. Provide pencils, crayons and vowel word cards.

2. Reproduce a copy of the "Pick Pocket Clown" on the following page for each player.

3. Write words that contain long or short vowel sounds on strips of tagboard. Place the strips in a shoe box.

Procedure:

1. This game is for any number of players.

2. The group is divided into two teams.

3. One player is selected to be the "caller."

4. The caller draws a word from the box and pronounces it.

5. The player must write the word on the clown's pocket.

6. The game continues until all the spaces on the clown's pockets are filled.

7. The caller checks the words to see if they are spelled correctly.

8. One point is given for each correctly spelled word.

9. The team with the most points wins the game.

Variation:
   Words can be used that contain long vowel sounds or dipthongs.

11

RED-HOT RULES

Purpose:

Using vowels, consonant clusters, prefixes, suffixes, and consonant digraphs

Preparation:

1. Provide markers and a die.

2. Reproduce a copy of the game board on the following page.

Procedure:

1. This game is for two, three or four players.

2. Each player places a marker on the game board.

3. The first player throws the die and moves the correct number of spaces. If the marker lands on a space marked "prefix," the player must spell a word which contains a prefix and so on.

4. The players continue until one player goes around the board three times to win the game.

13

CALLING ALL CONSONANTS

Purpose:

Using initial consonants

Preparation:

1. Provide paper and pencil.

2. Print one consonant on each of 21 index cards.

3. Reproduce a copy of the picture cards on the following page.

4. Cut the pictures apart and paste them on 21 index cards.

Procedure:

1. This game is for four or six players.

2. The cards are shuffled and dealt to the players.

3. The players check for pairs in their cards. A "pair" is a consonant card and a picture card that have the same beginning consonant sound. The pairs are placed on the table.

4. The first player draws a card from another player. If a matching card is drawn, the pair is placed on the table.

5. The players continue until all the cards have been drawn.

6. The players then write the names of the pictures in the pairs.

7. The player with the most correctly spelled pairs wins the game.

CALLING ALL CONSONANTS

ALPHABET ADVENTURE

Purpose:

Using initial consonants - vowels

Preparation:

1. Provide pencils, paper and crayons.

2. Reproduce a copy of the maze on the following page for each player.

Procedure:

1. This game is for any number of players.

2. Each player is given a maze, pencil, paper and crayons.

3. At a given signal, each player enters the maze with a crayon and draws a "path" to the first letter. The player draws a shape or object over the letter, and then writes a word that begins with that letter on the piece of paper. The word must contain at least five letters.

4. The players continue until one player completes the maze and wins the game.

Note:
The players may wish to color the maze or create a maze of their own for classmates to complete.

START

17

PERFECT ENDING

Purpose:

Using final consonants

Preparation:

1. Provide paper, pencils and tokens.

2. Reproduce a copy of the game board on the following page for each player.

3. Print different consonants on a copy of the game board.

4. Print vocabulary words according to reading level on colored construction paper. Place the words in a small box.

Procedure:

1. This game is for any number of players.

2. One player is selected to be the "caller."

3. All of the other players are given a copy of the game board, tokens, paper and pencil.

4. The caller draws a word from the box and pronounces it.

5. The other players look on their cards for the final consonant of the word called. If a player finds the letter, a token is placed in that space and the word is written on the paper.

6. The players continue until one player covers a complete row and calls "Perfect Ending."

7. The caller checks the words, and if they are spelled correctly, that player wins the game and becomes the next caller.

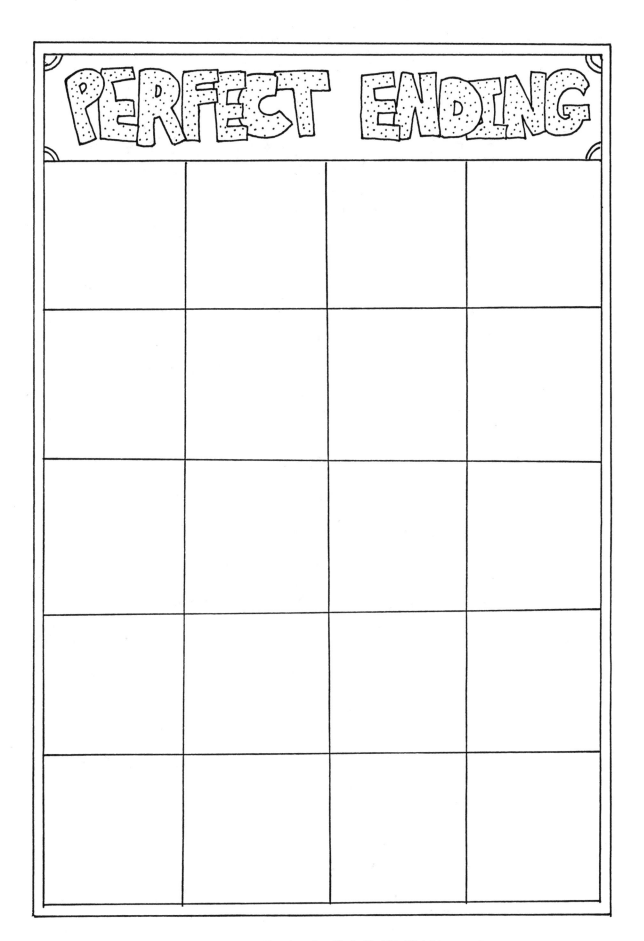

PERFECT ENDING

BLENDER'S BAG

Purpose:

Using consonant blends

Preparation:

1. Provide paper bag, pencils and paper.

2. Reproduce the consonant blend cards on the following page.

3. Cut apart the blend cards.

4. Place the cards in the bag.

Procedure:

1. This game is for any number of players.

2. Each player is given a piece of paper and pencil.

3. The "Consonant Blend Bag" is placed in the center of the players.

4. One player draws a blend card and holds it up for all the other players to see.

5. At a given signal, the players write as many words as possible that contain that blend.

6. The game continues until all of the blend cards have been used.

7. The player with the most correctly spelled words wins the game.

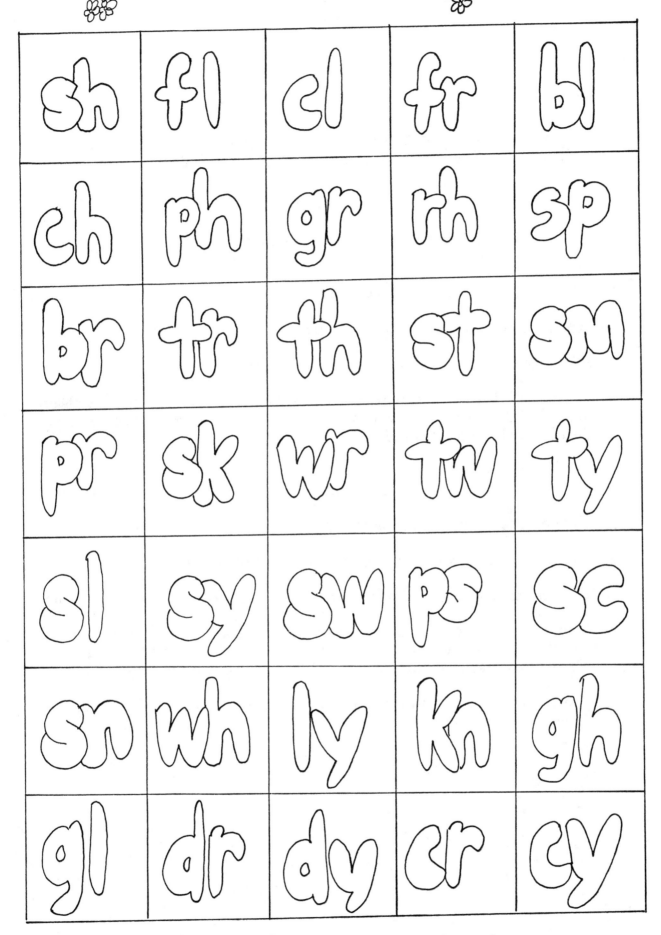

sh	fl	cl	fr	bl
ch	ph	gr	rh	sp
br	tr	th	st	sm
pr	sk	wr	tw	ty
sl	sy	sw	ps	sc
sn	wh	ly	kn	gh
gl	dr	dy	cr	cy

COMPUTER CRANNY

Purpose:

Using initial consonants - short vowels

Preparation:

1. Provide vowel spinner, pencils and paper.

2. Print one consonant on each of 21 index cards.

3. Cut a circle three inches in diameter from posterboard. Print the vowels on the circle. Cut an arrow from posterboard. Attach the arrow to the center of the circle with a metal brad.

Procedure:

1. The game is for two, three or four players.

2. The consonant cards are placed on top of a desk or table.

3. The first player selects a consonant card and then turns the vowel spinner.

4. All of the other players must write a word which begins with that consonant, plus the vowel on the vowel spinner, plus another consonant to form a word. (Example: consonant card "b", vowel "a" and consonant "t, d, or g".)

5. The players continue until one player has a total of 50 words to win the game.

  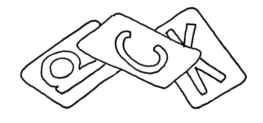 

FREAKY FORTUNES

Purpose:

Using present and past tense verbs

Preparation:

1. Cut off the top of a gallon-sized milk container. Cover the container with foil to resemble a crystal ball.

2. Print the following words on index cards.

grow	swam	drank	write	go	work	come	listen	run
did	play	ate	dug	see	take	start	fight	thought
throw	ring	have	drove	won	am	begin	forget	teach

3. Place the word cards in the crystal ball.

Procedure:

1. This game is for two, three or four players.

2. The first player draws a card from the crystal ball. If the card has a present tense word written on it, the player spells the past tense of the word. If the card has a past tense word on it, the player spells the present tense of the word. If the word is spelled correctly, the player keeps the card. If the word is misspelled, the player puts the card back into the crystal ball.

3. The game continues until all of the cards have been used.

4. The player with the most cards wins the game.

DOUBLE DUTY

Purpose:

Using suffixes

Preparation:

1. Provide word cards, markers, pencils and paper.

2. Reproduce a copy of the game board on the following page.

3. Print the following words on small squares of posterboard.

cut	sit	hit	mop	shine	plan	hop
have	bat	live	love	top	drive	spin
swim	fan	come	grin	stroke	bake	run

4. Prepare an answer key.

Procedure:

1. This game is for two players.

2. Each player places a marker on the game board.

3. The cards are shuffled and placed face down on the game board.

4. The first player draws a card and reads it aloud. The player adds the suffix "ing" to the word by doubling the last letter and adding "ing," or by dropping the last letter before adding "ing." The player spells the word aloud and then writes the word on a piece of paper. The player moves forward one space.

5. The game continues until one player reaches "finish."

6. The players check the answers with the answer key. The player with the most correct answers wins the game.

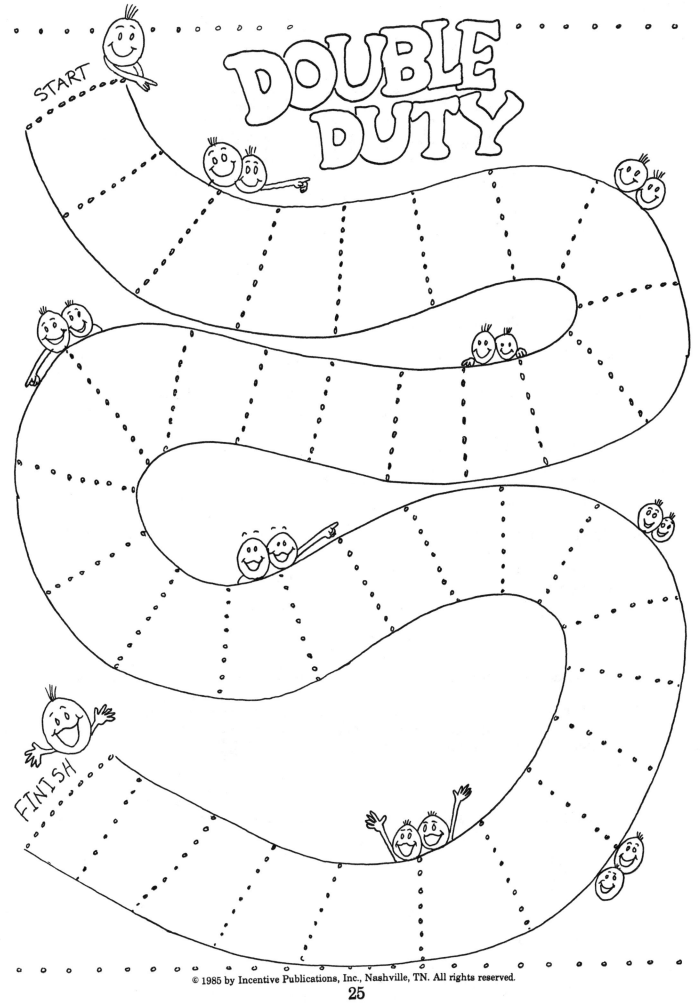

START

DOUBLE DUTY

FINISH

ABBREVIATED TREASURES

Purpose:

Using abbreviations

Preparation:

1. Provide pencils and crayons.

2. Reproduce a copy of the treasure chest on the following page for each player.

3. Prepare four lists of words to abbreviate. Use days of the week, months of the year, state names, professions and titles.

4. Roll up the word lists and tie with brightly colored ribbon.

5. Cover four shoe boxes with self-adhesive or gift wrapping paper to resemble treasure chests.

6. Place one word list in each box.

7. Prepare an answer key for each word list. Place the answer keys in envelopes and place one in each box.

Procedure:

1. This is a free-time activity and may be used by any number of students.

2. A student selects a box, takes out a word list, writes the abbreviation to each word on the treasure chest and checks the work using the answer key. The student then selects another box and follows the same procedure.

Note:
   The treasure chests make a nice bulletin board display.

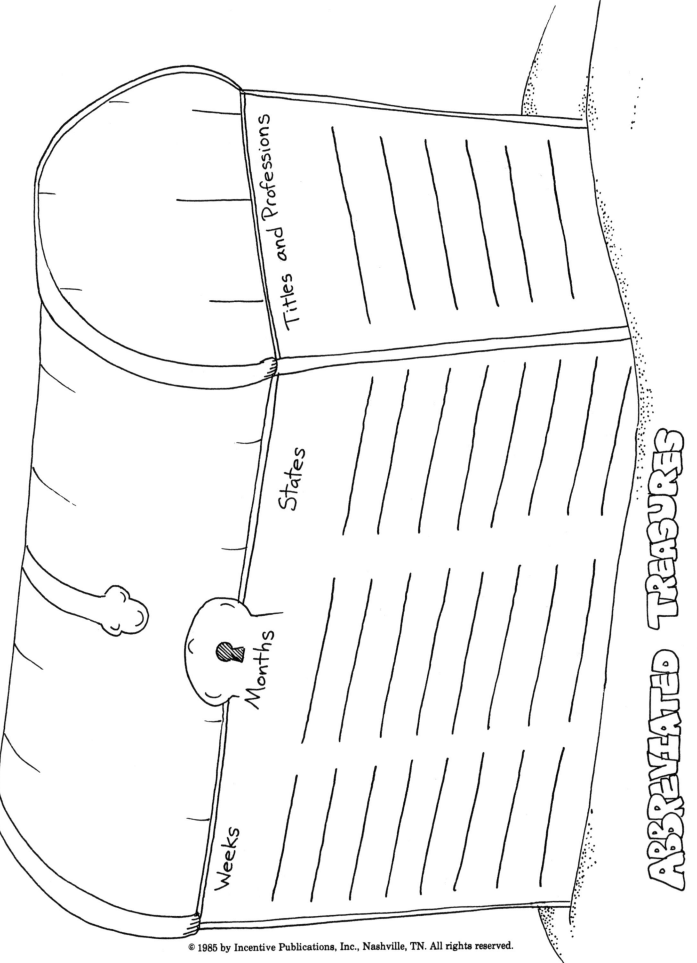

Titles and Professions

States

Months

Weeks

ABBREVIATED TREASURES

BRIEFLY STATED

Purpose:

Using abbreviations

Preparation:

1. Provide pencils.

2. Reproduce a copy of the map on the following page for each player.

3. Prepare a list of the 50 state names.

4. Prepare an answer key.

Procedure:

1. This game is for any number of players.

2. At a given signal, players try to identify each state and write its abbreviation on the correct space. (The list of state names can be used for reference.)

3. The first player to label the entire map with the correct abbreviations wins the game.

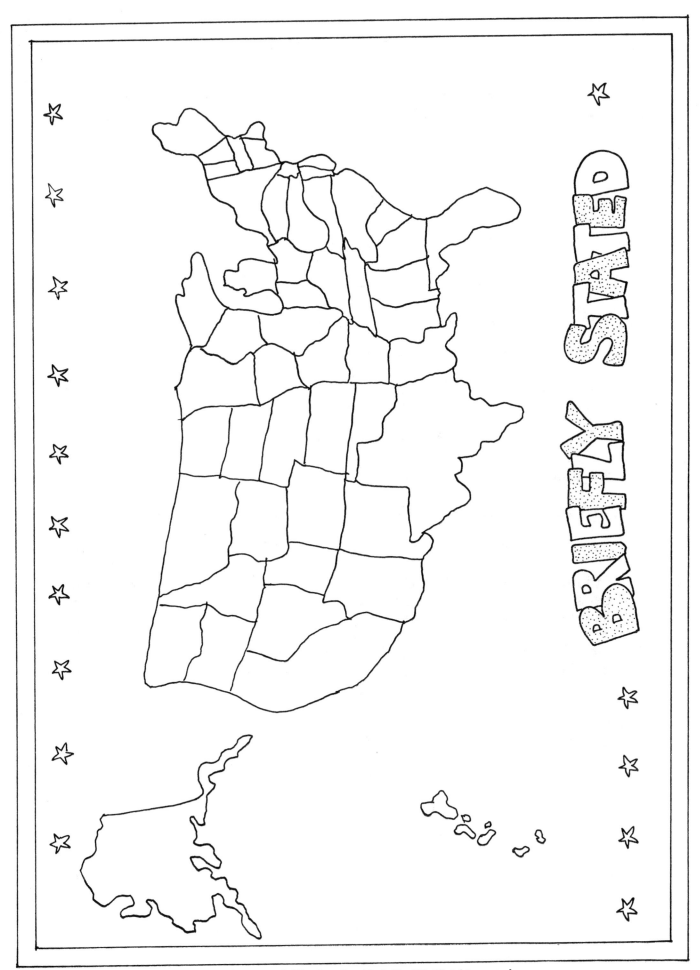

BRIEFLY STATED

CLASSY CONTRACTIONS

Purpose:

Using contractions

Preparation:

1. Provide word bottles, embroidery hoop, paper and pencils.

2. Reproduce a copy of the words on the following page.

3. Provide liter-sized soft drink bottles.

4. Tape the words on the bottles.

Procedure:

1. This game is for two players.

2. The bottles are placed in a triangular shape as bowling pins are arranged.

3. The first player tosses the hoop and tries to "ring a bottle."

4. If the bottle is ringed, the player pronounces the words on the bottle and spells the contraction for the words. If the contraction is spelled correctly, the player receives one point.

5. The game continues until all of the contractions have been spelled correctly. The player who has the most points wins the game.

Note:
   This game can be used as a special interest center.

You are	I have	have not
does not	should not	they are
is not	cannot	let us
it is	are not	will not

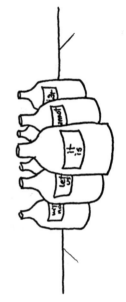

COMPOUND CORNER

Purpose:

Using compound words

Preparation:

1. Provide markers, pencils and a die.

2. Reproduce a copy of the game board on the following page.

Procedure:

1. This game is for two players.

2. The markers are placed on "start."

3. The first player throws the die and moves the correct number of spaces. Then the player writes a word on the game board to form a compound word.

4. The game continues until all of the spaces on the game board have been filled in.

5. The player with the most correctly spelled compound words wins the game.

Variation:

This game can be played by the entire class. The class is divided into two teams. Each student is given a copy of the game board. At a given signal, the two teams write words on the game board to form compound words. The first team whose members correctly spell all of the compound words on the game board wins the game.

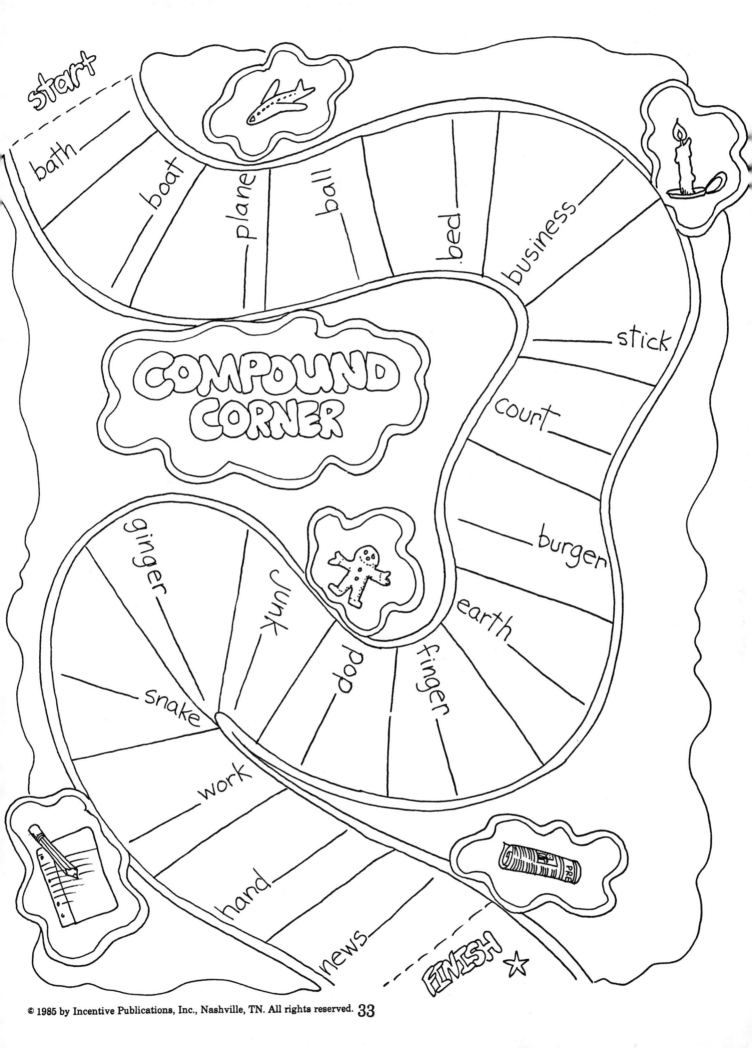

start

bath

boat

plane

ball

bed

business

stick

court

burger

COMPOUND CORNER

ginger

junk

pop

finger

earth

snake

work

hand

news

FINISH ☆

PLURAL PICNIC

Purpose:

Using plurals

Preparation:

1. Reproduce a copy of the picnic baskets on the following page for each player.

2. Provide scissors, glue, pencils, crayons and large pieces of manila drawing paper.

3. Prepare an answer key.

Procedure:

1. This game is for any number of players.

2. The players cut out the picnic baskets. The baskets are glued on the manila paper.

3. The players select a word from one of the picnic baskets and write its plural on the manila paper.

4. The game continues until all of the plurals of the words in the baskets have been written.

5. The players check the correct spelling of each word with the answer key.

6. The players color and decorate the manila paper to resemble a tablecloth with food or picnic baskets on it.

Note:
   The decorated "tablecloths" can be displayed on the bulletin board.

calf
mouse
cherry
tooth
bus

infant
radio
ox
donkey
lunch

igloo
inch
foot
fairy
wife

parent
grass
scientist
pilot
patio

spy
boy
child
knife
catch

pony
animal
sheep
balloon
tomato

book
city
deer
loaf
dictionary

story
fisherman
lamb
lily
brush

ROOT RELAY

Purpose:

Using root words or base words

Preparation:

1. Provide word cards, chalk and a small bell.

2. Reproduce the word cards on the following page.

3. Paste the words on a piece of tagboard. Cut the words apart to make cards.

Procedure:

1. This game is for any number of players.

2. The group is divided into two equal teams.

3. The word cards are shuffled and placed face down.

4. The teacher draws a card, reads the word and rings the bell.

5. One player from each team runs to the chalkboard and writes the root/base word and either the prefix or suffix. The first player to correctly spell the root/base word and prefix or suffix wins a point for the team.

6. The players continue until one team scores 20 points to win the game.

Variation:
Instead of the players writing the words on the chalkboard, they can write them on a piece of paper. The players would stand up when a base/root word and a prefix or suffix is written. The first player to stand wins a point for his or her team.

transplant	prefix	prepay	midair	profile
impure	misspell	inactive	television	uneven
unicycle	refinish	nonsmoker	overgrown	interact
readable	bakery	wooden	notify	artist
joyous	hopeless	goodness	athletic	beautiful
childhood	cleaner	longest	movement	protective

VARIETY VICTORY

Purpose:

Using antonyms, homonyms and synonyms

Preparation:

1. Provide word cards, markers and a die.

2. Reproduce a copy of the game board on the following page.

3. Print words that have antonyms, homonyms and synonyms on index cards.

Procedure:

1. This game is for two, three or four players.

2. Each player places a marker on the game board.

3. The word cards are placed in three stacks — antonyms, homonyms and synonyms.

4. The first player throws the die and moves the correct number of spaces. If the space is marked "A," the player draws an antonym card, pronounces the word and spells an antonym for the word written on the card. If the word is spelled correctly, the player stays on that space. If the word is misspelled, the player goes back two spaces.

5. The other players continue until one player goes around the board three times to win the game.

DARING DARTS

Purpose:

Using the weekly spelling list or other special list

Preparation:

1. Make a target using a black marker and heavy drawing paper.

2. Attach the target to a cork bulletin board.

3. Make darts using small pieces of wood and nails.

4. Cover four small boxes with gift wrapping paper or self-adhesive paper.

5. Print the numbers 1, 5, 10 and 15 on each box.

6. Print different spelling words on 24 small squares of tagboard. The spelling words should vary in level of difficulty.

7. The less difficult words should be placed in Box 1. Words a bit more difficult should be placed in Box 5. Words at the next level should be placed in Box 10, and the most difficult words should be placed in Box 15.

Procedure:

1. This game is for two, three or four players.

2. The first player throws a dart at the target. If the dart lands on 5, the player draws a card from Box 5 and pronounces that word. If the player can spell the word, he or she receives 5 points. The same format follows for the other boxes (i.e., 1 point for a word from Box 1 and 10 points for a word from Box 10).

3. The players continue until one player scores 30 points to win the game.

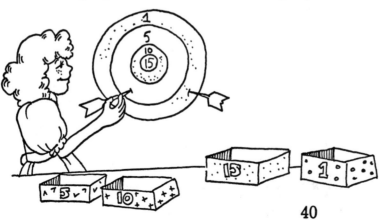

GREAT GUESSERS

Purpose:

Using a review spelling list or other special list

Preparation:

1. Provide word cards and masking tape.

2. Print review spelling words on index cards.

Procedure:

1. This game is for the entire class.

2. Tape a word card on the back of each player, but do not let the player see the word.

3. One player gives three clues about the word on the other player's back. If the player can guess the word and spell it correctly, the card is removed.

4. The game continues until all of the words have been identified and spelled correctly.

DAZZLING DETECTIVES

Purpose:

Using the weekly spelling list or other special list

Preparation:

1. Provide a kitchen timer, writing paper and pencils.

2. Make 30 magnifying glasses from tagboard using the pattern on the following page.

3. Write a spelling word on the underside of each magnifying glass.

4. Write a clue about the word on the top of each magnifying glass.

5. Arrange the magnifying glasses on the table to enable students to read the word clues.

Procedure:

1. This game is for two, three or four players.

2. The kitchen timer is set for ten minutes.

3. At a given signal, each player reads a word clue and writes the word on the paper.

4. The game continues until the timer stops.

5. The players check the correct spelling of the words on the undersides of the magnifying glasses.

6. The player with the most correctly spelled words wins the game.

DAZZLING DETECTIVES

RIGHT OR WRONG?

Purpose:

Using the weekly spelling list or other special list

Preparation:

1. Provide markers and word cards.

2. Reproduce a copy of the game board on the following page.

3. Print a variety of spelling words, or words from a spelling list on 20 index cards.

4. Print incorrectly spelled words from the same list on 20 index cards.

Procedure:

1. This game is for two, three or four players.

2. The cards are shuffled and placed face down beside the game board.

3. Each player places a marker on the game board.

4. The first player draws a card. The player must decide whether or not the word is spelled correctly. If the word is misspelled, the player must spell it correctly.

5. The player moves one space on the game board for each correct answer.

6. The players continue until one player reaches "finish" to win the game.

Variation:
   This game can be played without the use of a game board with the entire class.
   1. The class is divided into teams.
   2. The teacher writes a word that is either spelled correctly or incorrectly on the board.
   3. The players must decide whether the word is spelled correctly or incorrectly and write it on a piece of paper.
   4. The players continue until all of the words have been used. The team with the most correctly spelled words wins the game.

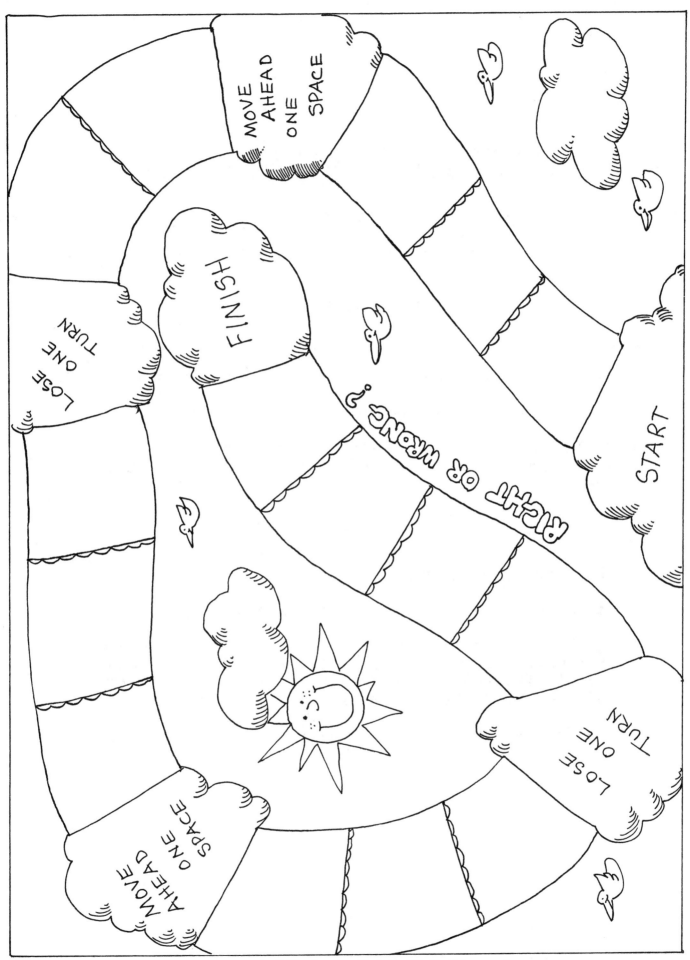

MOVE AHEAD ONE SPACE

FINISH

LOSE ONE TURN

RIGHT OR WRONG?

START

LOSE ONE TURN

MOVE AHEAD ONE SPACE

BOWLING BONANZA

Purpose:

Using the weekly spelling list or other special list

Preparation:

1. Provide pencils and "Bowling Bonanza" pins.

2. Reproduce a copy of the score sheet on the following page for each player.

3. Cut out 20 bowling pin shapes from colored posterboard.

4. Print the numbers 1-10 on two sets of pins. Print a word from the spelling list on the back of each pin, using the higher number for the more difficult words.

Procedure:

1. This game is for two players.

2. The bowling pins are placed face down in front of each player.

3. The first player says the number of a pin. The second player reads the word on the back. If the first player spells the word correctly, he or she knocks down the pin by picking it up and placing it in a pile. The second player then writes the word on the score sheet.

4. The player with the most pins wins the game.

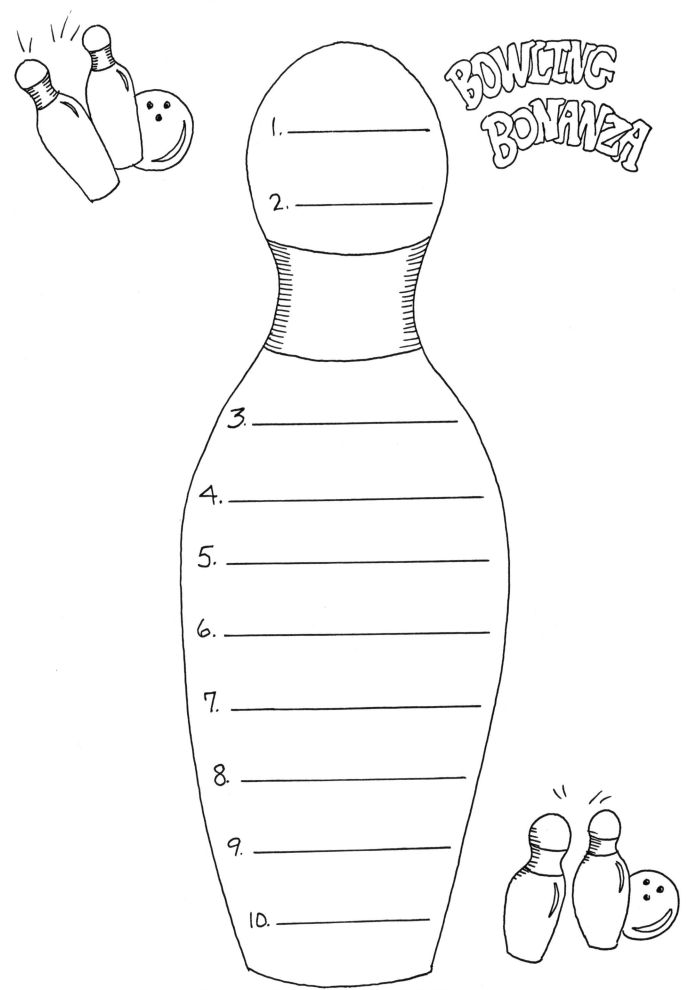

BOWLING BONANZA

1. _____
2. _____
3. _____
4. _____
5. _____
6. _____
7. _____
8. _____
9. _____
10. _____

CHECKER CRAZE

Purpose:

Using the weekly spelling list or other special list

Preparation:

1. Make 12 red and 12 black checkers from posterboard.

2. Reproduce a copy of the checkerboard on the following page.

3. Print a spelling word on the back of each checker.

Procedure:

1. This game is for two players.

2. The checkers are placed on the checkerboard.

3. The first player moves a checker, then the second player moves a checker. If a player can jump the other player's checker, he or she must spell the word which is under the checker. If the word is spelled correctly, the player may jump the checker and pick it up.

4. The game continues until one player is out of checkers. The player who still has some checkers left wins the game.

Note:
   A Spelling Checker Tournament would be fun for the class to hold.

CHECKER CRAZE

PARK AND LOCK

Purpose:

Using the weekly spelling list or other special list

Preparation:

1. Provide crayons and word cards.

2. Reproduce a copy of the parking lot on the following page for each player.

3. Print a variety of words on 30 index cards.

Procedure:

1. This game is for two players.

2. The word cards are shuffled and dealt to the players.

3. The first player draws a word card and pronounces the word to the second player. The second player spells the word. If the word is spelled correctly, the second player colors a car, truck or motorcycle in a parking space.

4. The game continues until all the words have been spelled. The player with the most cars, trucks or motorcycles in the parking lot wins the game.

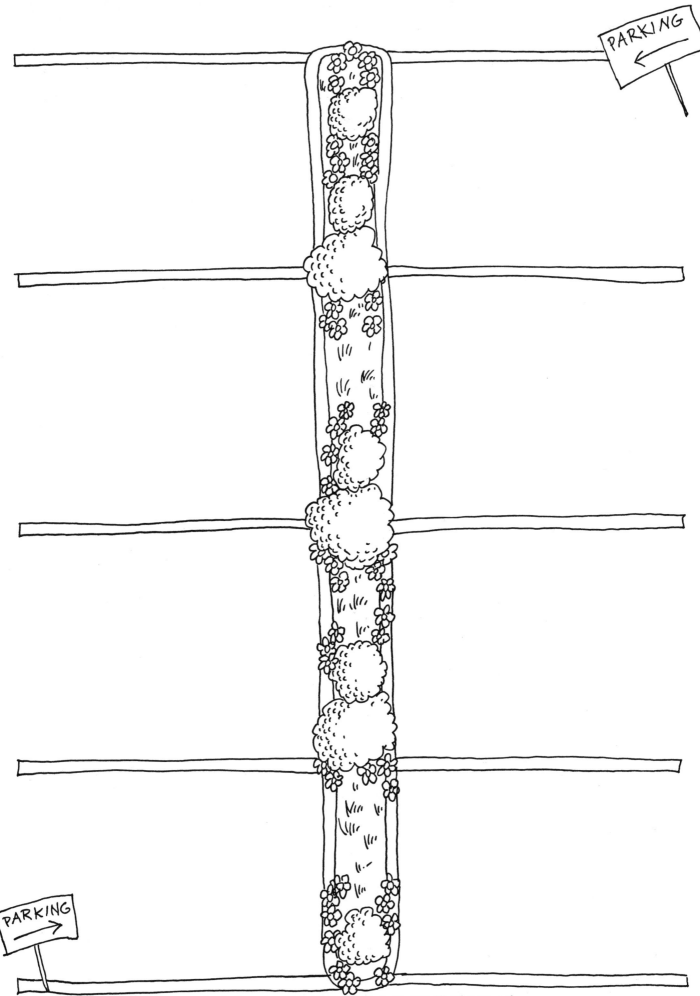

PARKING ←

PARKING →

TOUCHDOWN

Purpose:

Using a review spelling list or other special list

Preparation:

1. Provide brown construction paper, scissors and word cards.

2. Reproduce a copy of the game board on the following page.

3. Print review spelling words on index cards.

Procedure:

1. This game is for two players.

2. Each player cuts a football shape from construction paper to use as a marker.

3. The markers are placed on the game board on the 50 yard line.

4. Each player chooses a goal.

5. The first player draws a word card and pronounces the word. The second player tries to spell the word. If the word is spelled correctly, the player moves his or her football marker 10 yards. If the word is misspelled, the football marker is moved back 10 yards.

6. The first player to reach the goal line scores a touchdown to win the game.

Note:
This game is particularly fun to use during football season.

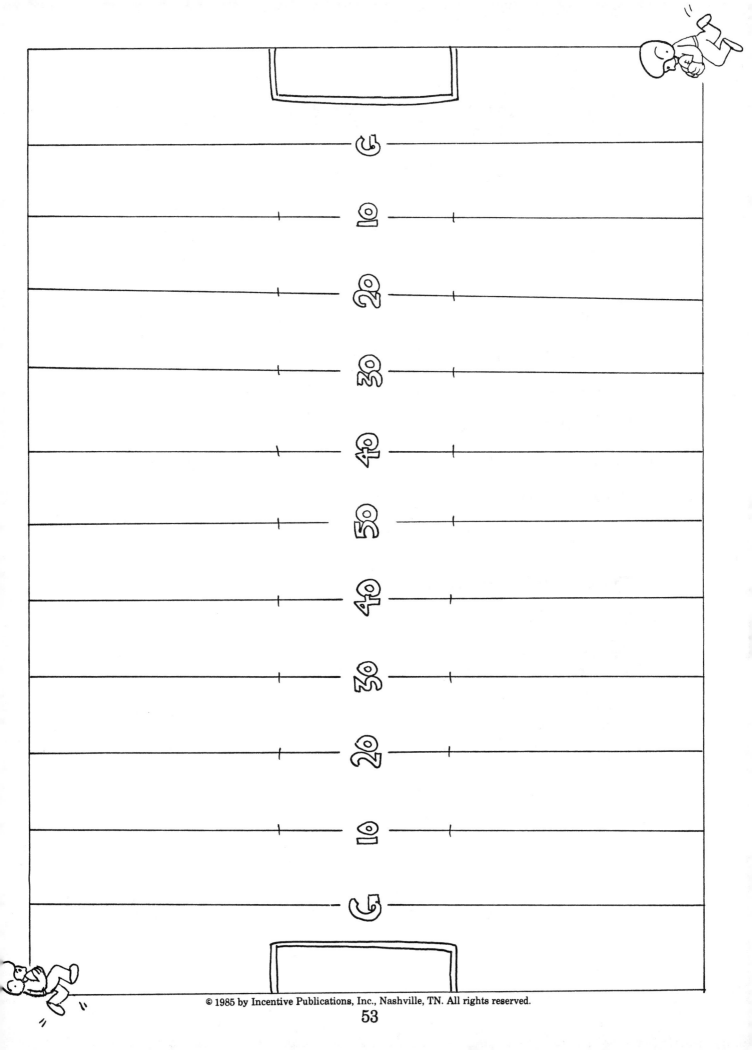

MOUNTAIN CLIMBERS

Purpose:

Using the weekly spelling list or other special list

Preparation:

1. Reproduce a copy of the mountain activity sheet on the following page for each player.

2. Cut an old sheet or fabric scraps into 30 2" x 6" strips.

3. Print a variety of spelling words on the strips with a felt-tip pen.

4. Provide two six-foot ropes.

5. Attach the word strips to the rope, with the most difficult words at the top.

6. Hang the ropes in the classroom doorway.

Procedure:

1. This game is for two players.

2. Each player selects a word rope.

3. The first player pronounces the first word on the rope. The second player starts climbing the mountain by writing that word on the activity sheet.

4. The game continues until all the words have been spelled correctly. The first player to reach the top of the mountain wins the game.

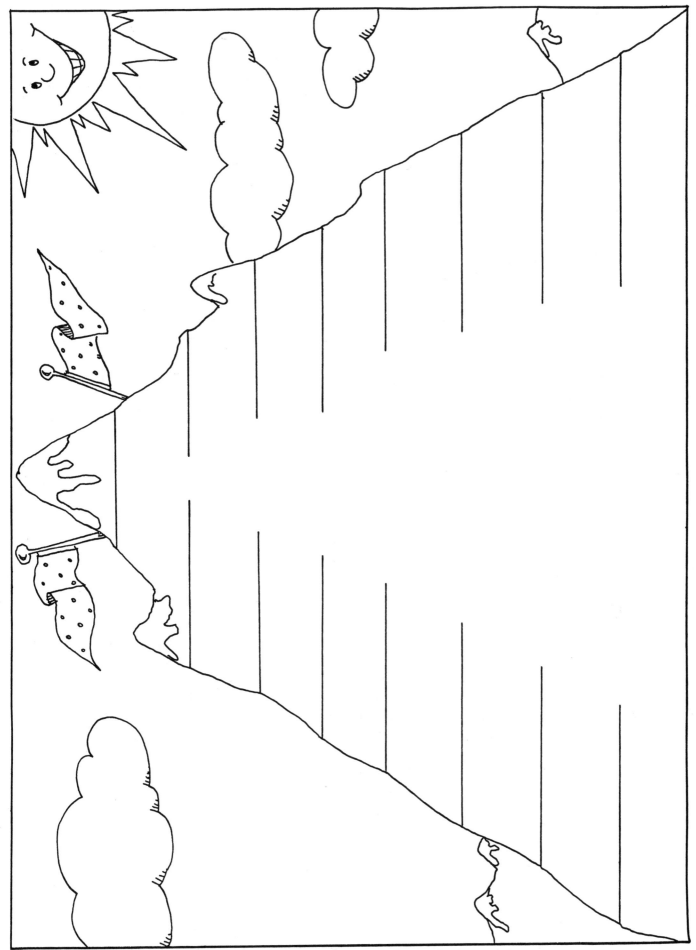

ALL STARS

Purpose:

Using the weekly spelling list or other special list

Preparation:

1. Provide word cards, construction paper and scissors.

2. Reproduce a copy of the game board on the following page.

3. Print "single hit" on five index cards; print "double" on five cards; print "triple" on five cards and print "home run" on five cards.

4. Print a spelling word on the back of each card. "Single hit" words should be the least difficult and "home run" words should be the most difficult.

Procedure:

1. This game is for any number of players.

2. Each player makes a marker from construction paper and places it on the game board.

3. The players are divided into two teams.

4. The word cards are placed in stacks on the game board.

5. The team who is "out in the field" draws a card and pronounces the word for the player who is "at bat." If the word is a "single hit" and the player spells it correctly, he or she goes to first base. If the word is a "triple" and the player spells it correctly, he or she goes to third base and so on. If a word is misspelled, it is an "out." Three outs and the other team gets a chance to bat.

6. The players continue until nine innings have been played, and the team with the most runs wins the game.

PUZZLING PIECES

Purpose:

Using the weekly spelling list or other special list

Preparation:

1. Provide pencils and crayons.

2. Reproduce a copy of the puzzle on the following page.

3. Paste a copy of the puzzle on a piece of tagboard. Cut the puzzle into pieces.

4. Write the definitions of words that are related to a current unit, or spelling words on the backs of the puzzle pieces.

5. Prepare an answer key.

Procedure:

1. This game is for the entire class or for two players.

2. The first player draws a puzzle piece, reads the definition and writes the word on the blank side of the puzzle. If the word is spelled correctly, the puzzle piece is placed on a desk. If the word is misspelled, the puzzle piece is placed back with the other puzzle pieces.

3. The players continue until all of the words have been spelled correctly.

4. The players then fit the puzzle pieces together.

Note:
Students may want to draw a picture over the puzzle pieces.

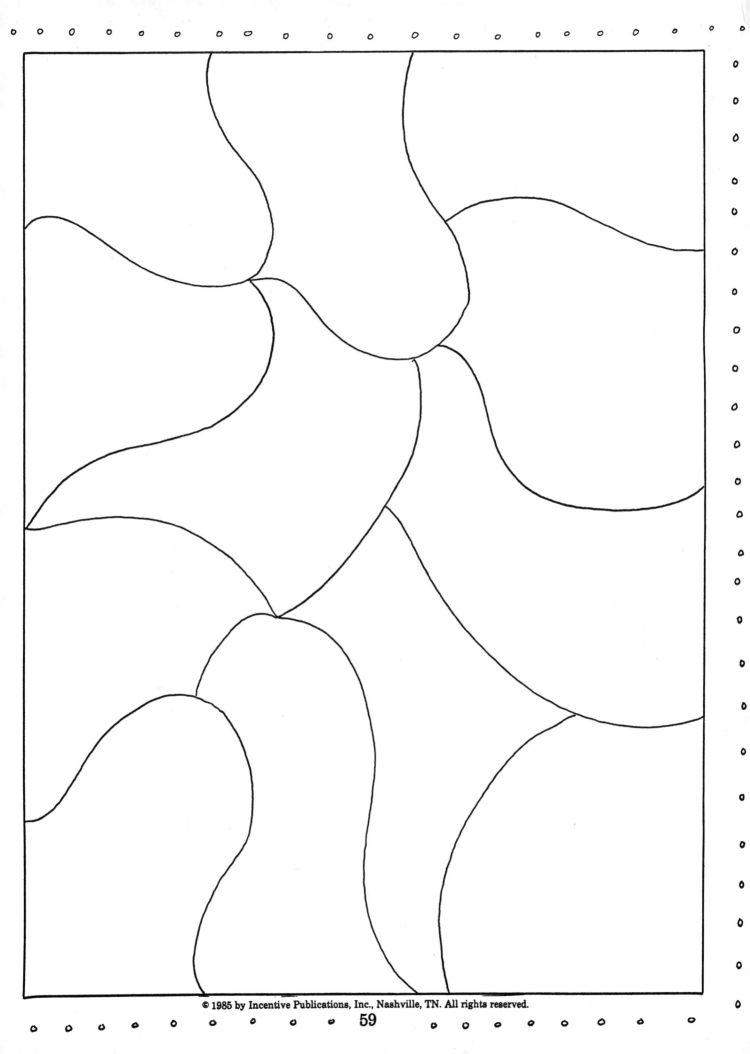

SPEECH SPLASH

Purpose:

Using parts of speech

Preparation:

1. Provide markers and a die.

2. Reproduce a copy of the game board on the following page.

Procedure:

1. This game is for two or more players.

2. Each player places a marker on the game board.

3. The first player throws the die and moves the correct number of spaces. If the player's marker lands on the space marked "noun," the player spells a word that is a noun and so on.

4. The game continues until one player goes around the board three times by spelling the words correctly to win the game.

ANIMAL ANSWERS

Purpose:

Using parts of speech (nouns) or special words

Preparation:

1. Provide markers and cards.

2. Reproduce a copy of the game board on the following page for each player.

3. Print "one" on ten index cards; print "two" on five index cards; print "three" on three index cards; print "go back one space" on two index cards; print "move ahead one space" on four index cards.

Procedure:

1. This game is for two or more players.

2. Each player places a marker on "Zoo Entrance."

3. The cards are shuffled and placed face down.

4. The first player draws a card and moves the correct number of spaces. The player must correctly spell the name of the animal in the space. Then the player must spell the name of an animal that does not live in a zoo, but whose name begins with the same letter as the zoo animal.

5. If the names of the animals are misspelled, the player must go back to the last starting position.

6. The other players continue until one player reaches "Zoo Exit" to win the game.

Variation:
Players can also spell the colors, species, foods eaten or names of animals' babies.

ANIMAL ANSWERS

MAP MAKERS

Purpose:

Using words related to subject areas

Preparation:

1. Provide a world map and pencils.

2. Reproduce a copy of the "Map Maker's Guide" on the following page for each player.

3. Use the following list of words:

equator	degrees	southern	continent	ocean	mountain
latitude	hemisphere	eastern	country	river	legend
longitude	northern	western	island	lake	gulf

Other words may be added according to grade level.

Procedure:

1. This game is for the entire class.

2. The class is divided into two teams.

3. The teacher selects a word from the list and points to it on the world map.

4. The students write the name of the item the teacher is pointing to on the "Map Maker's Guide."

5. The players continue until all the words have been spelled. The team who spells the most words correctly wins the game.

MAP MAKER'S GUIDE

1. _____   11. _____

2. _____   12. _____

3. _____   13. _____

4. _____   14. _____

5. _____   15. _____

6. _____   16. _____

7. _____   17. _____

8. _____   18. _____

9. _____   19. _____

10. _____   20. _____

SHAKE AND MAKE

Purpose:

Making words from letters

Preparation:

1. Provide two jars, kitchen timer, scissors, paste and construction paper.

2. Reproduce the letters on the following page for each player.

Procedure:

1. This game is for two players.

2. Each player pastes one set of letters on a piece of construction paper and cuts out the letters. One set of letters is then placed in each jar.

3. The kitchen timer is set for three minutes.

4. The players shake the jars and spill out the letters.

5. Each player then tries to make as many words as possible within the three minute period.

6. Three-letter words count three points, four-letter words count four points and five-letter words count five points.

7. The remaining letters are placed in the jars and the game continues until one player has 20 points to win the game.

Variation:
   This game can be played with the entire class. Each player has a set of cut-out letters. At a given signal, the players try to make as many words as possible. At the end of a three minute period, the players count their words. The player who has the most words wins the game.

MATH MONSTER

Purpose:

Using cardinal numbers

Preparation:

1. Provide math problem cards, paper and markers.

2. Reproduce a copy of the game board on the following page.

3. Write addition, subtraction, multiplication and division problems according to grade level on 40 index cards.

Procedure:

1. This game is for two, three or four players.

2. Each player places a marker on "start."

3. The math cards are shuffled and placed face down.

4. The first player draws a card and solves the math problem on a piece of paper. The player spells the answer to the problem. (Example: 28 + 35 = 63, the player spells s-i-x-t-y t-h-r-e-e.)

5. If the word is spelled correctly, the player moves one space on the game board. If the word is misspelled, the player remains on that space.

6. The other players continue until one player reaches the Math Monster to win the game.

STAR GAZERS

Purpose:

Using rhyming words

Preparation:

1. Cut out 20 stars of different sizes from yellow construction paper.

2. Write words on the stars that can be matched easily to a rhyming word.

3. Hang the stars from the ceiling.

4. Reproduce a copy of the star on the following page for each player.

5. Provide an answer key.

Procedure:

1. This game is for any number of players.

2. The players choose a star, and write as many rhyming words as they can on the large star. The players then check the correct spelling with the answer key.

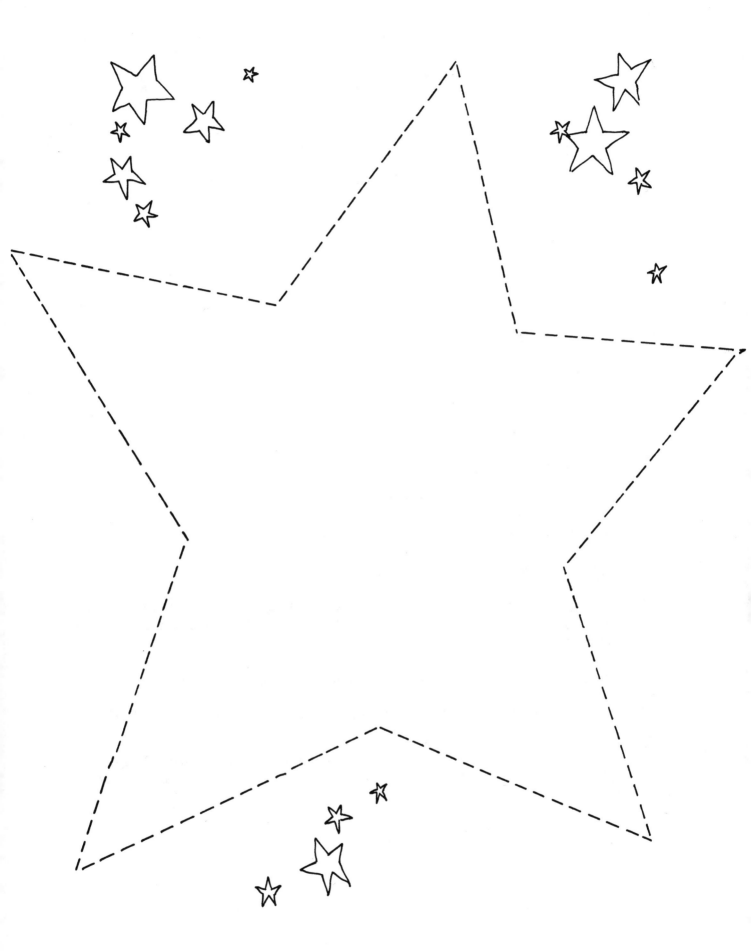

CATEGORY CAPERS

Purpose:

Practicing spelling commonly used words

Preparation:

1. Provide category cards in envelopes.

2. Print words from the categories listed on the following page on index cards.

3. Place the word cards in envelopes.

4. Label the envelopes according to the category.

Procedure:

1. This game is for the entire class.

2. The players are divided into teams of six.

3. One player is selected to be the leader on each team.

4. The teams take turns selecting categories.

5. The leader draws a card from the selected category and pronounces the word. One member of the team must spell the word. If the word is misspelled, another team may spell the word.

6. One point is given to the team for each correctly spelled word.

7. The game continues until one team scores 15 points to win the game.

Note:
   The category words may be changed to make the words more or less difficult to spell or other categories may be used. Examples: countries, states, months, etc.

FOODS	COMMUNICATION	SPORTS	TRANSPORTATION	CLOTHING
cereal	Braille	boxing	space shuttle	kimono
bread	homing pigeons	fencing	helicopter	muumuu
milk	sign language	tennis	airplane	spacesuit
steak	satellites	wrestling	tugboat	turban
fish	smoke signals	archery	ocean liner	tunic
hamburger	drumbeats	bowling	yacht	kilt
chicken	typewriter	golf	canoe	cloak
potato	telegraph	swimming	dirigible	beret
tomato	pony express	baseball	ambulance	fez
carrot	radio	basketball	kayak	sombrero
lettuce	television	football	raft	slipper
beans	video tape	soccer	travois	bonnet
cucumber	newspaper	ice hockey	dog sled	vest
apple	hieroglyphics	rugby	covered wagon	stockings
grapefruit	movies	fishing	balloon	overcoat
orange	computers	boating	clipper ship	Mackinaw
banana	conversation	canoeing	unicycle	trousers
lemon	telephone	skiing	automobile	jerkin
spaghetti	records	track	stagecoach	jeans
cantaloupe	books	volleyball	railroad	evening dress

LOOK AND SPELL

Purpose:

Practicing spelling commonly used words

Preparation:

1. Provide picture cards and pencils.

2. Reproduce a "Look and Spell Record Page" on the following page for each player.

3. Cut out small pictures of various objects from a catalog.

4. Paste the pictures on index cards.

Procedure:

1. This game is for two players.

2. The picture cards are dealt and placed face down.

3. At a given signal, each player draws a picture card and writes the word on the record page.

4. The players continue until all of the cards have been used.

5. The first player to finish and correctly spell all of the words wins the game.

LOOK & SPELL
RECORD PAGE

1. _____

2. _____

3. _____

4. _____

5. _____

6. _____

7. _____

8. _____

9. _____

10. _____

11. _____

12. _____

13. _____

14. _____

15. _____

16. _____

17. _____

18. _____

SPELLING STORIES

Purpose:

Practicing spelling commonly used words

Preparation:

1. Provide word strips, pencils and crayons.

2. Reproduce a copy of the "Spelling Story Sheet" on the following page.

3. Print words from a spelling list on strips of tagboard.

Procedure:

1. The game is for two players.

2. The first player draws a word strip and writes a sentence with that word to begin a story.

3. The second player draws a word strip and writes the next sentence in the story.

4. The players continue to draw words and write sentences until the story is completed.

Note:
   The players may want to illustrate their stories or read them aloud to the class. The stories may also be displayed on the bulletin board.

SPELLING STORY SHEET

SIGHT SEEING

Purpose:

Practicing spelling commonly used words

Preparation:

1. Provide word cards, paper and pencils.

2. Reproduce a copy of the tour bus on the following page for each player.

3. Print the following words on index cards:

airport	factory	museum	ship	university
bridge	garden	ocean	statue	zoo
building	hospital	park	synagogue	institution
church	mountain	river	temple	lake

Procedure:

1. This game is for any number of players.

2. The word cards are shuffled and placed face down.

3. The first player draws a word card, pronounces the word and the other players write the word on the tour bus.

4. The game continues until all of the words have been spelled.

5. The player who has the most correctly spelled words wins the game.

Variation:
 The monthly or six week's review spelling list may be used.

Note:
 The buses can be colored and displayed on the bulletin board.

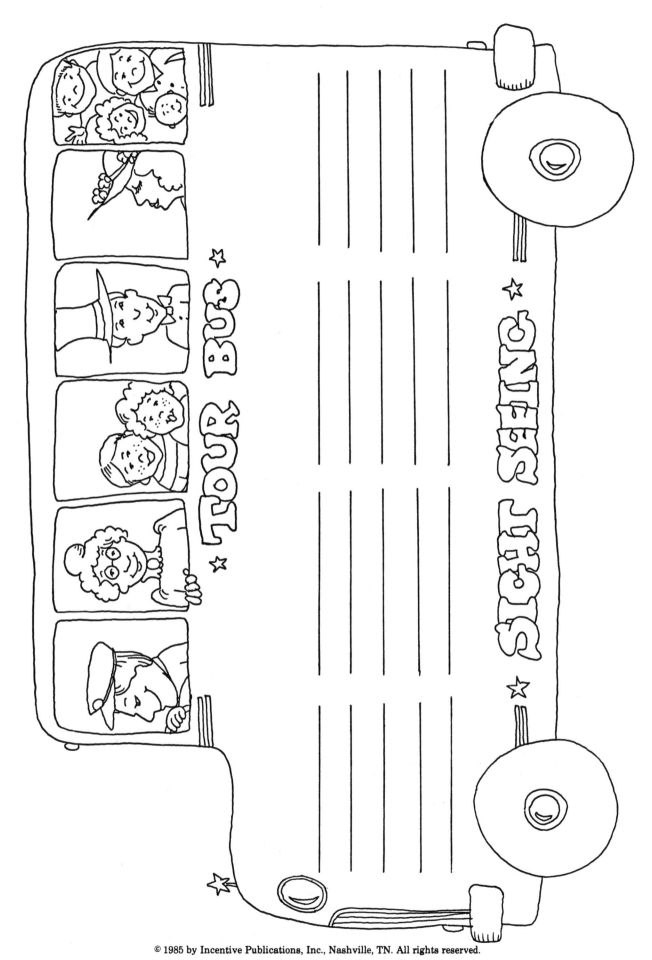

HOLIDAY HUNT

Purpose:

Practicing spelling commonly used words

Preparation:

1. Provide markers.

2. Reproduce a copy of the game board on the following page.

3. Make a spinner using posterboard and a brass fastener. Print the numbers 1 and 2 on the spinner.

Procedure:

1. This game is for any number of players.

2. Each player places a marker on "start."

3. The first player spins and moves the correct number of spaces.

4. The player spells the holiday that the picture represents.

5. If the holiday is misspelled, the player loses one turn.

6. The game continues until one player reaches "finish" to win the game.

Variation:
   Players may be asked to identify one other symbol commonly associated with the holiday. (Example: Thanksgiving/turkey, and spell the name of the holiday and the symbol.)

PICTURE PLAY

Purpose:

Practicing spelling commonly used words

Preparation:

1. Reproduce a copy of the game board on the following page.

2. Provide markers and a die.

Procedure:

1. This game is for two, three or four players.

2. Each player places a marker on "start."

3. The first player throws the die and moves the correct number of spaces.

4. The player must spell a word from the category on which the die landed.

5. If the word is spelled correctly, the player keeps the marker on the space. If the word is misspelled, the player must go back two spaces.

6. The other players continue until one player reaches "finish" to win the game.

Variation:
   Word categories from a current unit can be used for this game.

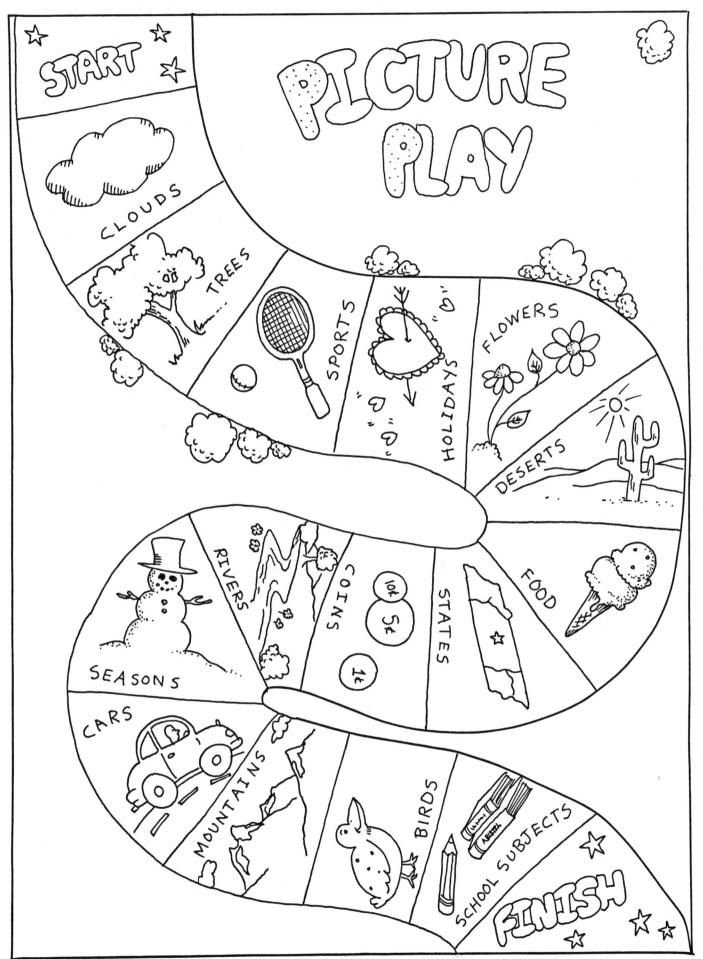

SPELLING SPREE

Purpose:

Practicing spelling commonly used words

Preparation:

1. Provide pencils and catalogs.

2. Reproduce a copy of the order form on the following page for each player.

Procedure:

1. This game is for any number of players.

2. The first player selects an item from a catalog, pronounces its name and tells what page it is on. The other players write the name of the item and the page number on the order form.

3. The game continues until the order form is complete.

4. The players check the correct spelling of each word with the catalog description. The player with the most correctly spelled words wins the game.

ORDER FORM

ITEM

PAGE

1. _____ _____

2. _____ _____

3. _____ _____

4. _____ _____

5. _____ _____

6. _____ _____

7. _____ _____

8. _____ _____

9. _____ _____

10. _____ _____

11. _____ _____

12. _____ _____

13. _____ _____

SPELLING SPREE

CALENDAR CLUES

Purpose:

Practicing spelling commonly used words

Preparation:

1. Reproduce a copy of the calendar.

2. Provide paper, pencil and a small cube.

Procedure:

1. This game is for two or four players and may be used as a free-time activity.

2. The first player tosses the cube on the calendar. The player must spell aloud the day of the week on which the cube lands. Then the player must write the day of the week on which the cube lands.

3. The first player must also spell the date aloud.

4. If the day of the week is spelled correctly, one point is given. If the date number is spelled correctly, two points are received.

5. The players continue until one player receives 15 points to win the game.

Variation:
This game can also be used to spell the cardinal numbers by using addition. The first player tosses the cube on the calendar. The player adds six to the number on which the cube lands. (Any number can be added.) Then the player spells aloud the total of the two numbers.

CALENDAR CLUES

S	M	T	W	T	F	S
	1	2	3	4	5	
6	7	8	9	10	11	12
13	14	15	16	17	18	19
20	21	22	23	24	25	26
27	28	29	30			

APPENDIX

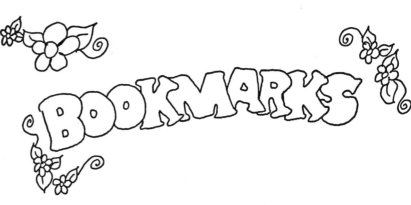

BOOKMARKS

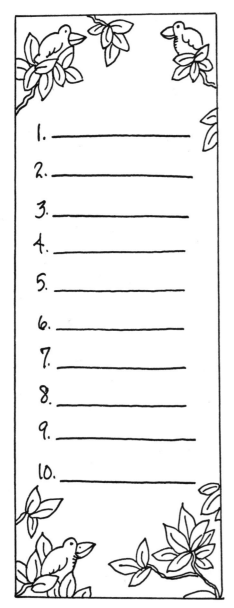

1. _____
2. _____
3. _____
4. _____
5. _____
6. _____
7. _____
8. _____
9. _____
10. _____

Reproduce the following bookmarks for students to use to write weekly spelling lists on, so they will see the words at a glance.

SPELL IT WELL!

1. _____
2. _____
3. _____
4. _____
5. _____
6. _____
7. _____
8. _____
9. _____
10. _____

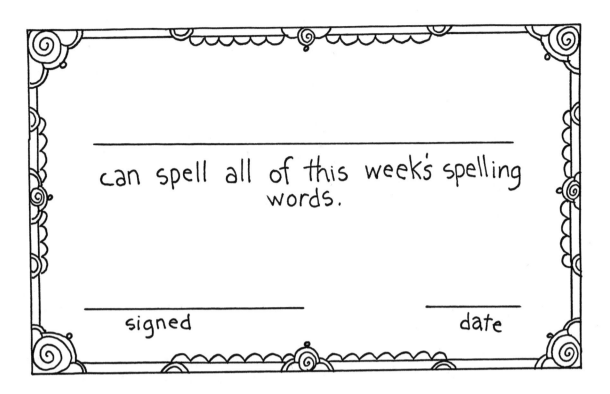

_____

can spell all of this week's spelling
words.

_____   _____
signed   date

SPELLING REWARDS

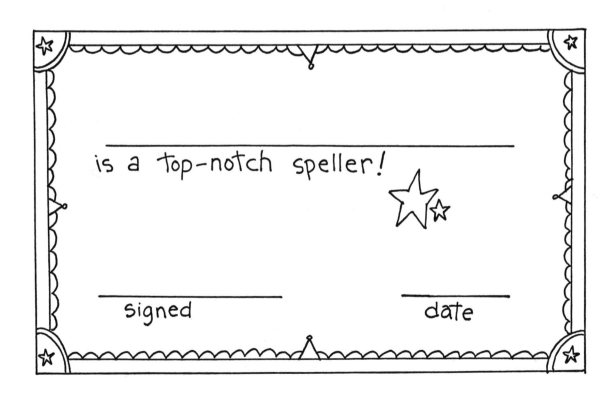

_____

is a top-notch speller!

_____   _____
signed   date

TEN WAYS TO REINFORCE SPELLING SKILLS

1. Set aside a time each week for an old-fashioned spelling match. Designate the words in advance so students can study the words beforehand.

2. Have students make a box of words that are troublesome to them. Students can exchange boxes with a friend to make learning the words more fun.

3. Primary or slow learners can make picture dictionaries by writing the spelling word alongside a picture of the item.

4. Write a word of the day on the chalkboard. Students can try to commit the word to memory by speaking and writing it throughout the day.

5. Students try to find ten words in their library books that are unfamiliar to them. Then, they look up their meaning in the dictionary and learn how to spell them.

6. Students can have a word hunt using their science and social studies books. Students make illustrated lists of 10 to 15 words they are not able to spell that interest them.

7. Have a spelling scramble with this week's spelling words by dividing the class into two teams. The first team to unscramble all the words wins!

8. Reinforce the week's spelling list by giving only clues to the words. The students must try to guess and spell the correct word from the clues given.

9. Make mobiles of the week's spelling list to hang around the room. These will serve as constant reminders of the words students need to learn.

10. Have students cut out pictures of items with synonyms and learn to spell both words (Example: sun, son; pear, pair).

SPELLING RULES

The following spelling rules are generalizations, and do not work all of the time. However, they are often true, and are valuable spelling aids.

1. Each syllable of a word must contain one sounded vowel. (al li ga tor)

2. A vowel is more likely to be pronounced short than long.

3. A vowel at the end of a one-syllable word is usually long. (be)

4. The final *e* in a one-syllable word is usually silent. (lake)

5. When *i* precedes *gh*, it is usually long. (bright)

6. *I* comes before *e* except after *c*, or when sounded like *a* as in *neighbor* and *weigh*. (chief, receive)

7. Usually, a doubled consonant or vowel has one sound. (letter, boot)

8. When two vowels are together, the first one usually says its own name. (team)

9. The *ch* sound is often spelled *tch*. (catch)

10. The *j* sound is often spelled *dg* or *dge*. (dredging, smudge)

11. The *k* sound may be made by *c* or *ck*. (came, stack)

12. The *gh* combination is usually silent (dough, fright) but sometimes it sounds like *f*. (trough, laugh)

13. The consonants *c* and *g* are soft before *i, e,* and *y;* otherwise, they are hard. (go, gentle; center, car)

14. The ending *-ance* may also be spelled *-ence*. (endurance, presence)

15. The ending *-ous* may be used with an *e* or an *i*. (ominous, extraneous, delicious)

16. The ending *-tion* may be spelled *-cian, sian, sion,* or *-tian*. (station, physician, Prussian, decision, Dalmatian)

17. Pluralize a word that ends in *y* with a consonant before it by changing the *y* to *i* and adding *es*. (cry, cries)

18. The common prefixes *en-, in-,* and *un-* are not used interchangeably.

*Used by permission from **The Yellow Pages for Students and Teachers**
Copyright © 1980 by Incentive Publications, Inc., Nashville, TN.

SPELLING DEMONS

absence
accept
accessible
accommodate
acknowledgment
acquaintance
acquire
across
address
affect
all right
already
among
analysis
apparent
appearance
arrangement
attendance
author
balance
begin
beginning
belief
beneficial
benefit
benefited
breathe
business
calendar
canceled
career
category
ceiling
cemetery
changeable
chief
clothes
column
coming
commission
commit
commitment
committed
committee
conceive
confident

conscientious
control
convenience
convenient
criticism
criticize
curiosity
decide
decision
definite
definitely
description
desperate
develop
different
disappear
disappoint
doesn't
easily
effect
eligible
embarrass
endeavor
environment
equipped
especially
excellent
except
exercise
exhilarate
existence
experience
experiment
explanation
extremely
fascinate
February
finally
foreign
friend
further
generally
government
grammar
grateful
guarantee

guard
height
heroes
hoping
immediately
incidentally
incredible
independent
intelligence
interest
irrelevant
island
its
jealous
judgment
knowledge
laboratory
length
license
losing
maintenance
meant
medicine
necessary
neighbor
neither
nickel
niece
ninth
occasion
occurred
occurrence
omission
omitted
opinion
opportunity
original
paid
parallel
particularly
perceive
perform
personal
planned
possession
possibility

practical
practically
practice
preferred
principal
privilege
probably
procedure
proceed
pursue
questionnaire
really
receipt
receive
recommend
reference
referred
responsibility
rhythm
safety
schedule
secretary
seize
separate
several
shoulder
significant
similar
sincerely
socially
stationary
stationery
succeed
surprise
temporarily
therefore
thorough
through
tragedy
undoubtedly
until
using
usually
Wednesday
weird
writing